Bruce is not well.
He will not eat.
He looks sad.
The children are taking
him to the vet.
A vet is an animal doctor.

In the waiting-room
are people with their pets.
A tabby cat has a bad tooth.

A parrot has broken a wing.
A rabbit needs to have
its claws cut.

Here comes the nurse.
She helps the vet.
She takes Bruce into a room
called the Surgery.
Everything is very clean.
It is like being in a hospital.

The vet has spent many years
learning about animals.
She knows how they should
be fed and housed.
She knows what to do
when they are ill.

Bruce is put on the X-ray machine.
This machine takes pictures
of the inside of his body.
They show he needs
a small operation.

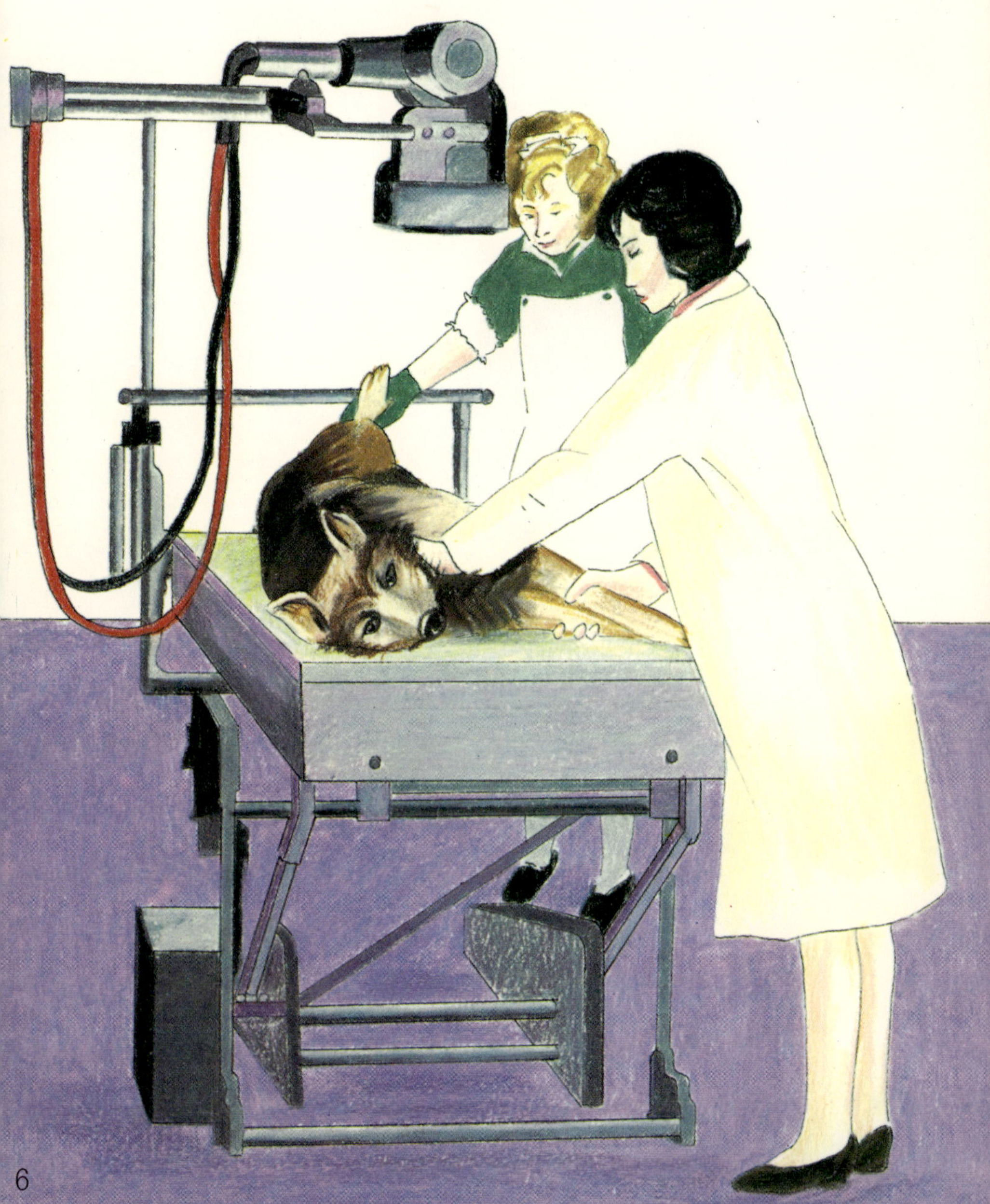

The children say goodbye
and leave him with the vet.
When it is time for his operation
the nurse places Bruce
on the operating table.
Soon he is in a deep sleep.

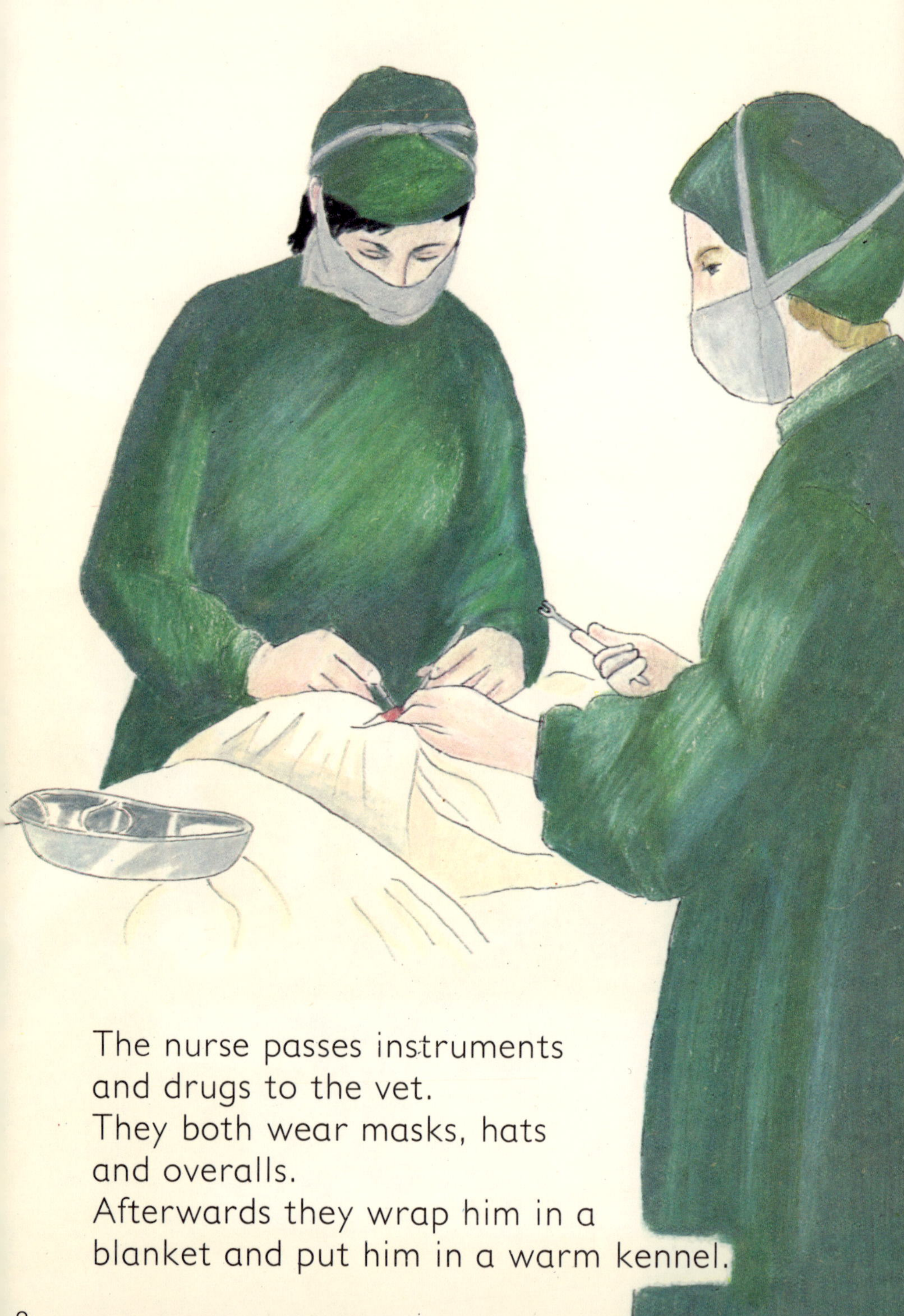

The nurse passes instruments
and drugs to the vet.
They both wear masks, hats
and overalls.
Afterwards they wrap him in a
blanket and put him in a warm kennel.

Next day the vet takes Bruce
home in her car.
The children are pleased
to see their dog again.
He is happy and well now.

Then she visits animals
who are too ill to visit her.
They may want pills, powders
or bottles of medicine.
These can be mixed in their food
or drinking water.

These two budgies have colds.
The vet gives them medicine
mixed with bird seed.
They will eat it and get better.

This poodle was hit by a lorry.
The vet went at once.
She bathed a bad cut
and stitched it.
If an animal is very ill,
She will go out during the night.

A horse in this old shed
has had a foal.
The vet stays to see
that they are alright.
Her only light comes from
a small lamp.

A lot of her work is on farms.
Cattle, pigs and sheep are tested
for diseases.
When they are ill
she tells the farmer
how to look after them.

The vet must be careful
not to spread a disease.
Before making her next call
her instruments are cleaned.
Her oilskin coat, rubber apron
and rubber boots are hosed down.

Some vets do other kinds of work.
Let's look at them.
This man inspects places
where animals are kept.
He is making sure
that the sheep at the market
are not badly treated.

Here a vet watches swill
being cooked.
Swill is the food given to pigs.
He checks to see that it is boiled
for a long time.
This kills the germs
which make pigs ill.

Dairies too must be inspected.
They should be really clean
and have healthy cows.
Then the milk they sell
will do us good.

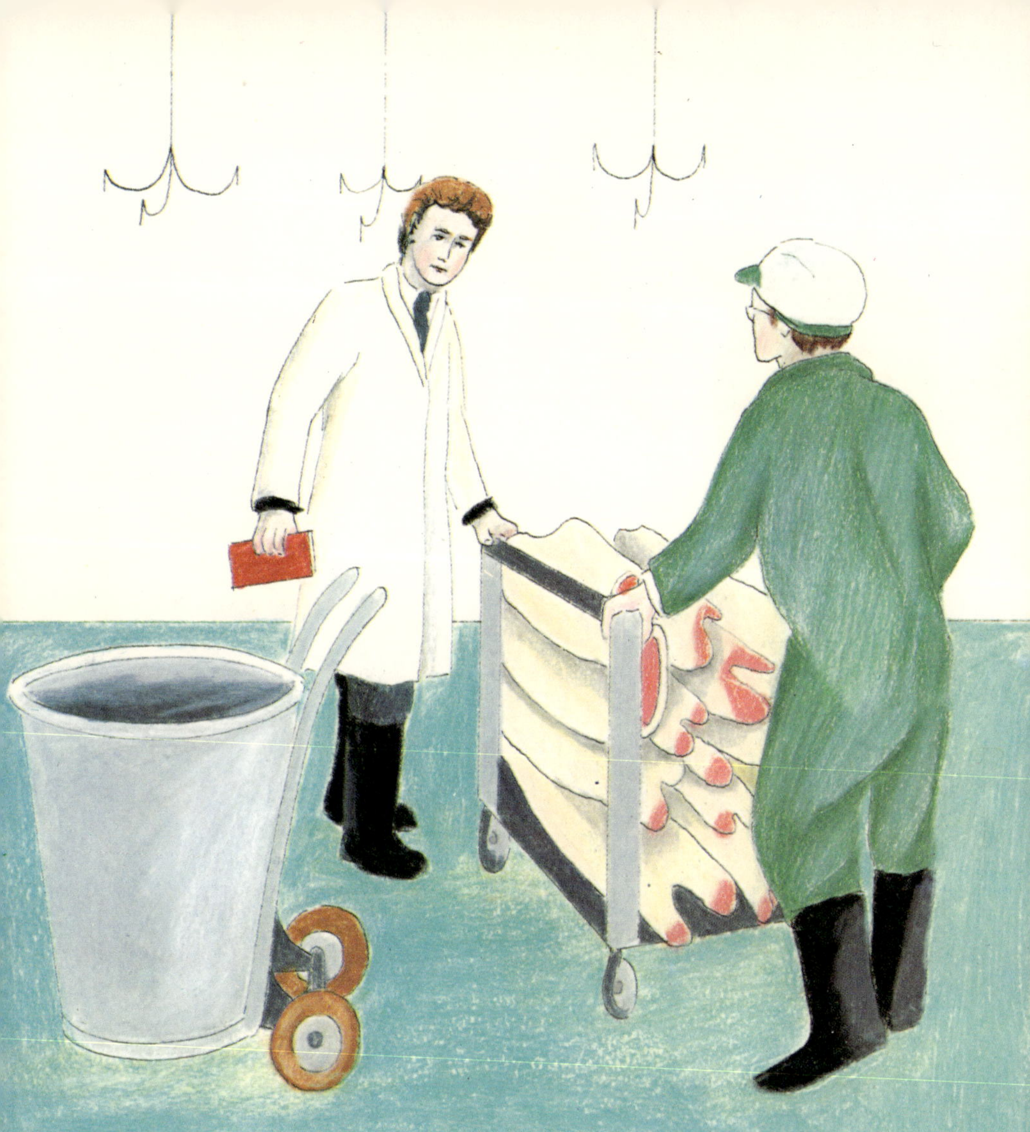

Meat is kept here.
As the men carry it in
the vet inspects it
to see that it is safe to eat.
Later some of it will go
to be sold in butchers' shops.

Zoo vets care for all kinds
of wild and dangerous animals.
They may weigh a few tons
or just a few ounces.
They come from all parts of the world.

The rhino is strong and unfriendly.
To get near him a dart gun is fired.
The dart will hit his body
and send him to sleep.

Then he can have his operation.

The keeper helps the zoo vet and so can we. See the notice on the cage? What does it say?

It is unkind to give animals
the wrong sort of food.
Then they become sick and too fat.

The circus has come to town!
While the animals are here
the vet will keep them well.
When the animals do clever trick
the children laugh and clap.

A. CHOOSE THE RIGHT ANSWER AND WRITE IT DOWN.

1. An animal doctor is called a (nurse, vet, keeper).
2. Bruce had an (apron, operation, overall).
3. The vet took Bruce home in her (hat, mask, car).
4. A foal is a baby (parrot, horse, sheep).
5. Pigs are fed on (seeds, pills, swill).
6. Cows are found in (dairies, kennels, shops).
7. The rhino is a (small, strong, happy) animal.
8. Circus animals do many (clever, clap, colds) tricks.

Check your answers against those on the back page.

B. NOW ANSWER THESE QUESTIONS. SOMETIMES A SENTENCE IS NEEDED.

1. When are pets taken to the vet?
2. What does an X-ray machine do?
3. Write two things which a vet may need during an operation.
4. Name three things which are cleaned after visiting the farm.
5. Why is pigs' swill boiled for a long time?
6. Which vet uses a dart gun?
7. What does it say on the zoo notice?
8. Draw a picture of your favourite pet. Write two sentences about it.

C. THINGS TO DO

1. Write a funny story or act a play about a vet and a talking parrot.
2. Make your own Pet Book. Stick in pictures and drawings. Write about them. At the back make a list of zoo animals.
3. Collect pet food cartons. Display them on a table or pinned to the wall.
4. Accidents happen when dogs run into roads. Paint a picture of two children taking their dog out on a lead.

ANSWERS.

1. vet 2. operation 3. car
4. horse 5. swill 6. dairies
7. strong 8. clever

D. THINGS TO FIND OUT.

1. How many children in your class have pets?
   Write down what they are.
2. Make a graph to show which pet is the most popular.
   Stick it in your Pet Book.
3. A foal is a baby horse.
   What do we call a baby-
   a) sheep b) cat c) cow d) dog?
4. What do these letters stand for?
   R.S.P.C.A.
   Vet is short for..........
   If you don't know ask your teacher.